A Theory of Roots

Homage to Boyd Hill Nature Preserve

Vincent Spina

NeoPoiesis Press, LLC

2775 Harbor Ave SW, Suite D, Seattle, WA 98126-2138
Inquiries: Info@NeoPoiesisPress.com
NeoPoiesisPress.com

Vincent Spina – A Theory of Roots
ISBN 979-8-9858336-1-4 (paperback: alk. paper))

    1. Poetry. I. Spina, Vincent. II. A Theory of Roots.

First Edition

Cover painting: Shara Bunis

Printed in the United States of America.

Dedicated to Donna Heinrich

In Memoriam

Contents

Boyd Hill Nature Preserve

I

According to the map on the wall
of the Education Center, the watershed
measures 2200 acres; the lake, Lake Maggiore
occupies 380 acres of it. Boyd Hill Nature Preserve
sits at the southern edge of the lake
and continues up the western bank:
a strip of unbroken green, narrowing
as it winds northward.

There is also a definition of what
makes a watershed: a sort of catch basin
where all the surrounding rivers, streams…
and flood runoffs commingle
to form a body of water: this lake.

The City of St. Petersburg, its white towers
gleaming toward the East, surrounds
the watershed, so that we may only guess
at what the land once looked like: perhaps
a repetition of cypress swamps, rich in nutrients
—prime farmland once the original growth
could be removed—punctuated by upland hammocks
or two, with the entrances of gopher tortoise
tunnels, where small reptiles and mammals
can take shelter.

And the lake:
Salt Lake once. More bayou than lake where
the fresh water streams twice daily mixed
with the salt tides of Tampa Bay.

The first people to arrive fished here,
returning to the lake what they could
for what they took out: a life of reciprocity and balance.
As early as the 1500s, Europeans realized a profit could be made.
Sports fisherman could be enticed to cast lines here. Thus, they
dammed the entrance
where the two waters met.
Mullet from the bay survived.
Introduced tilapia thrived.

II

The white towers of St. Petersburg
—the city's complex of old Southern mansions,
pockets of Section 8 Housing, newly rising
middle-class developments—press tightly
against the east bank of Lake Maggiore
and upwards along the east border of the watershed.

Along the Lakeside Trail, the towers gleam
through breaks in the entanglement of strangler fig trees,
palmettos and, further down, clumps of cattail.

Self-assured, the towers reach upwards,
a product of human hands—black, white…hands
of immigrant-refugees from Central America,
both "legal" and "illegal". Sky cranes, perched atop
newly rising edifices, lift and lower cables,
like the spinnerets of a mother spider, too vast
in scale for the human mind
to conceive.

Up and down the trail
the towers are a presence
and I think of lines from John Ashbery's "These Lacustrine Cities":
        …grew out of loathing
            Into something forgetful, although angry with history,
            Burning until that hate was transformed into useless love".

Is it loathing then that causes these towers to gleam,
an architect's vision solidifies in concrete and steel,
financed through the schemes of developers
and bankers, green for profit…and the need
of folk for shelter and to grow?

Moorhens sift through water vegetation for
sustenance, a green heron hunts, still as a statue,
waiting; alligators bask on the banks absorbing
energy from the sun. Cooters and softshell turtles
float weightless through murky waters. Farther
from the banks live oaks grow in the stillness
of ancient vegetation.

Ashbery continues, "You have built a mountain of something"
…something of human dimension, a shadow growing
at the edge of this once salt lake.

III

Halfway around the five kilometer trek
you come across the live oak, massive
in its stillness; the nature preserve itself pauses here,
comes to rest before it may pick up again.

A bench
placed in front of the tree bears a plaque:
a boy scout troop placed it here in memory
of their scout master…it is a good place to be remembered
and to remember.

I come and sit here
as often as I can…sometimes just to rest
at the midpoint of the trek, but often to assuage old griefs:
issues with my father, say, that were never resolved,
words that were never spoken ("The past is never dead.
It's not even past": Faulkner),

...as was the case with his father (which I witnessed
myself but was too young to understand): griefs,
inherited, in turn, bequeathed: father to son;
mother to daughter.

As often as not
someone else has beaten me to the bench,
reading, writing in a notebook, scrolling on a cellphone, perhaps,
feeling a grief of his or her own. Different causes,
but the grief is always the same: this or that soul,
suddenly conscious of its essential nakedness,
a son of Noah and Noah at one and the same time
—the nakedness deep, drunken, and unremitting.

There is a kind of knowledge
(or even wisdom) in the tree's very stillness
...not of mind but stored in its very DNA,
growing richer, fibrous, and more complex over epochs
of evolution, coming to terms with fire
that both destroys and creates, and with water
that both destroys and creates.
It is mostly in what is vegetable,
but in creatures that live long lives,
elephants, whales, turtles.

You feel it in the branches
of this live oak that jut out horizontal to the trunk
over twenty or thirty feet, gently arching down
to touch the ground
as if to bear the weight of all these years, these epochs.

Rising from the bench
and turning to the tree I can't help but to feel the living quality
of the bark, wrinkled like the hide of some vast creature,
more than plant, more than animal, but organic in essence:
the stillness of becoming, the wisdom of stillness.

I come here, as often as not,
for this tree.

IV

From the Live Oak, the 5k trail circles back
to the Center. Quartz run-off from the ever diminishing
Appalachian Range mingles with the coral sand
from Florida's many journeys from sea bottom
to recovery as dry land. The state changes: wet to dry,
a sort of breathing. The Preserve changes in accordance

Slash pines replace live oak...are replaced
by scrub palmettos. White sand, which cannot retain
the rainfall from the wet season, replaces the rich loam
along the Lakeside Trail...
a desert of sorts where gopher tortoises
find it easy to dig tunnels. Freshly brought-up sand mark
the entrances: a keystone species. Small mammals
and reptiles find refuge here from the summer heat,
the winter chill...and I think of turtles

—the only pet I was allowed in a city apartment,
red-eared sliders I loved and killed so well for lack of understanding
of their needs—

...and the wisdom of turtles:
gravid loggerheads and leatherbacks journeying
thousands of miles to lay a clutch of eggs on the very beaches
where they themselves hatched: a secure place to which
their very lives attest...box turtles that hardly ever leave
a certain woodland range—a sort of home, they relentlessly
try to return to, if taken out...a snapping turtle laden
with eggs will not turn back no matter how many times
one risks a finger to prevent her from crossing a dangerous road

...and this need to find a secure place to lay a clutch of eggs, or
in which to live...a wisdom, not solely of mind...as if 200 million
years of evolution had embedded it into the DNA, the shell itself,
the very fiber of the muscles, to which the mind adds a certain
memory of sight, taste, and smell...and this persistence
to return...as if a map laid out in their being could not rest
until a certain analogue were found in the terrain...not

9

exact, of course…and then a sense of security rises,
a sort of dawn…

as if this need to secure the safety of a clutch of eggs
could morph someday (even in another species) into a need
to secure the safety of the hatchlings…and this would be a step
toward a need to care…which could be a step toward love

…just as if a need to live in a secure place were the prime
condition to base a notion of happiness. I think back

to the myriad "journeys to recovery" I've trekked.
A therapist asked me if my "interest" in turtles could rise
from my own need to escape into a shell… Perhaps…sure…
later it occurs to me: this persistence to return…to find
the right place.

On one side of the trail a fence separates the Preserve
from soccer fields, a golf court, some upscale housing.
On the other, the saw palmetto, the gopher tunnels

and I think
of one individual, perhaps, whose analogue in the terrain
lies on the other side of the fence.

Addendum

One night in spring, nearby the Education Center,
the water boils around the body of a bull gator
as he roars out rage and passion

...and someone who hears beyond the Center
rises from bed, goes to an open window
and closes it, wondering what crazy fool
is revving a Harley motor at two in the morning.

And That Yellow Flower

I

…and that yellow flower
more yellow for being alone and seen alone
emerging from the deep-green of swamp foliage
and merging with it….still mirror

of those yellow butterflies
that flicker on and off like random ghosts
in search of something (but what?) through the upper boughs
of the cypress trees, raising knees through the soil
like *shan shui* mountains in a banzai landscape

and just beyond
rising on small island-hammocks of solid soil,
the live oaks, strangler figs and their usual victims,
the cabbage palms:

a merging of time and place—this moment of stillness
in movement: a name, a way, the way a serpent
emerging from the mouth of a Toltec God
becomes a tongue, and the tongue is speech, is power.

Can you see
what I'm getting at: the yellow flower,
the thing, and the thing's in-itself, which is process
before and after and during the thing…and the naming
which seems never to catch up
or the simple morning-glory that becomes
the glory of morning…can you see?
And you? and me?

II

...as simple as an after-dinner walk
when a wisp of spider thread lightly brushes
across your forehead, and your way
has just crossed the silk road
the creature has left as a "breath of air"
—hardly perceived—floating
through space. Yes,

it is here and it is now
and the sorrow too—frozen...still—
as when a caring arm resting across your shoulders
helps you to rise from the cushioned kneeler
and you turn for one last, lasting look
as the lid of the casket is gently lowered. What

is the name for this cup constantly spilling over
and of these places and times that flow seamlessly
one into the other? A seed becoming a flower,
the life of a larva that becomes a ghost searching
though the upper levels of the dense, green canopy

The glory of morning
and the evening shadow

Bull Alligator

Yes, it is true. In my long lifetime
I have eaten more than one of my children.

In the words of the one who puts words
in my mouth, I make no apologies,
nor do I boast or take pride in this fact.
It is true, they were softer to bite into
than the shells of slider and cooter turtles,
though one or two may have bit my tongue
as I swallowed. Otherwise,

my meals are mostly bluegills,
the fat tilapia new to these waters,
a moorhen, raccoon, or someone's pet
naive enough… In the words of the one who
puts words in my mouth…you know the rest.

I doze in the reed banks of slow moving brooks
in springtime. I roar like a revving Harley
at the scent-trail of my mates' pheromones.
She will build a nest-mound. Hatchlings will hatch.

I thank the morning sun who brings life
back to my limbs chilled in the winter night.

Inhuman, you might say? Perhaps.
…More like a god

Palm

The palm at the end of the mind: "Of Mere being"
~ *Wallace Stevens*

I think of a palm, and the history
of palms, and all it would tell us
if we could learn to say…and

that one unscheduled moment
while traveling between the many stops
assigned to a morning, assigned to peace.
No one is looking now. No conductor
to issue or collect a ticket. Here,

the only violence is the violence of life
intent on remaining alive: the ospreys
at their nest; the shrike outraged
by their existence…a fish. We say it is good.
We have no choice, would not be here
otherwise. And now, here,

a palm ornamenting a front lawn
or standing alone on a beach or
as a sign of water in oceans of sand
…simply being…here among
other palms as are bicyclists
going by on the Canal Trail

unconscious as the day is long, and,
we may add, "easy"…as easy
as a piece of cake, or a love slipped
under a pillow you we may dream about
later…easy as a palm grows. I want you

this way and me this way, and
the moment to continue this way.

Cypress Knees

And yet they are still there, sucked upward
out of the muck of humus and fossil sand

(a sea was here once…now a precarious swamp
abiding until the sea might return)

a city of mountains you might see in a Chinese ink
on silk tucked into the Asian section of a museum,

but in miniature, fetal. still uninhabited
…the science out on their purpose;

appendage lungs to the tree, like mangrove roots
bringing air to the mangrove growing in the airless mud(?)
anchors to the cypresses themselves
in this ambivalent time between land and flood(?)

…hope for no specific time or something,
no something at all, just a hope

seen for the first time now
once again.

A Theory of Roots

Hours will have passed…have already…
aligning themselves into years…volumes
of time…but to what extent
…to what end:

the "day" you are walking along the otherwise
carefully groomed Lakeside Trail and
heading north and just before the small
wooden bridge…you stumble
over a network of roots. A massive
strangler fig has laid down a labyrinth
of sorts rising from the base of the tree
on the west side of the trail and sinking back
at the other. And this concerns you

…or rather, you and, somehow, the roots have become
the focus of a concern that, rising from nowhere, seemingly,
suddenly contains you while, at the same time,
leaves you out: a restless twisting and turning
of the living fiber, observed for an instant,
then gone, tunneling through the soil,
gathering sustenance, churning
up the grains of sand and loam,
the dead and molding matter, as though,
farfetched as it may be, it were a rich brown
and granular cream slowly, infinitesimally slowly,
being churned into and even richer
butter   much the way,

but at this vegetal scale, fingers,
crazy in love, knead and caress
a breast. No words, exactly,

but there it is once again…
in these so-called knees of a cypress
that spring up from the soil—mirrors
on a dwarf scale to those mountains in Chinese paintings
rising from mist-drowned valleys—*shan shui*—

"mountain water" they are called. You saw
them once in a museum behind glass casings
and here they rise from earth and a top blanket
of dead palmetto fronds
and crisp brown live-oak leaves.

Thinking or not thinking at all,
it all seems to fit (or is it the constant desire
to make things fit?) whirling about, but slowly,
very slowly: a sort of fractal, this complexity, or
complicity of pieces joining together, falling apart
of the organic and the mineral, the caress
of the root running through soil and all
that is becoming root or is returning
to soil…

…may some day be a theory
—from vegetal root to human caress—
a principle of organization appears or seems to,
a plan neither wholly here nor wholly not here
at the same time and place…something
to be rounded up or wrapped into an equation
worked out on a mathematician's chalkboard
…or becomes the object of a lover's
obscure desire.

And at Tampa Bay, whose brackish waters
once mixed with Lake Maggiore, a path dead-ends
among mangroves. And this *concern*
that contains you while leaving you out
radiates into the roots of these mangroves
that raise the whole tree above the oxygen deprived mud
(otherwise potentially alive with what the land drains
into the sea and what the sea renders in exchange)
and, in this way, the tree breathes. It all seems clear now
though just beyond the boundaries of an explanation:

this breathing of the plant and of the tide
ebbing and flowing as if a pump's machinations
were at work…which is exactly what it is: the attraction

of moon to earth, earth to moon: a love affair
on a universal level...imagined? Real? And now.

how the low tide draws out the fiddler crabs
endlessly waving their one oversized claw
to the sun, attracting a mate,
warning a rival,

and how the high tide brings in
a random shark pup to find refuge
among the mangrove roots, from pelagic hunters
before it too becomes
a pelagic hunter

...and this play of predator and prey,
the breathing-in and breathing-out of earth and moon
may someday become a theory or prayer
—"why hast thou abandoned me"...
"into thy hands I commend my spirit"—
and where and how

it begins as a seed...the way a seed
of a strangler fig tree nestles
in a hollow of another tree, germinates
into thin vines that reach downward to earth
where they take root becoming vine and root and
how the veins multiply, widen around the tree, reach
down becoming more roots and join each other
around the tree until the tree disappears
within the labyrinth of veins and roots
as the fig tree kills while meaning
no harm, so that lovers
of figs may come someday
to eat the fruit

...the way some vague and hardly felt sensation
(such as the touch of sunlight or moonlight
on the skin of the great-grandparent
of your great-grandparent) takes root

in an old man you have known all your life
and never known whose gaze is now focused
on the pigeons he has raised his whole life
and he is one in their flight
above him

or in the face of an old women whom equally
you have known and not known
as she discovers for the first time the beauty
of a river she has crossed and recrossed
her whole life

and grows in a letter you are writing
or in the play of a certain color
you paint on a wall or a canvas
or in a melody you hum to yourself,
a color or melody you mold in clay
or sculpt from stone
or carved in wood

a theory you devise…a desire

Preserve

Though it is easier to forget
or not even realize, the purple and yellow
fire hydrant makes it clear

that this miniature cypress swamp,
the hammocks of live oaks and palms,
groves of laurel and live oak, are here

at the indulgence of other concerns
—a fluke on the maps of subdivisions;
a site too close to the mud and moods
of a lake, to be worth the investment.

Whatever the purpose, this measure
of osprey nests, tortoise tunnels,
a mother gator with her black and gold-striped
hatchlings may remain or be taken away,

While a labyrinth of buried pipes connects
the hydrant to the City's system of water
control, reminding the casual passerby
this imposed system is here to stay...

Others
—sons and daughters of a faith now
buried in raised mounds ignored
by time—also built: a bridge here or there
to cross a small arroyo to arrive
at a landing for dugouts—wood
the earth could reabsorb
once they were gone.

But here we are anyway—this small, green
intermission between concrete roads, lawns
and golf course—free to take a photo
of a father carrying his sleepy child
over one of these carefully plotted trails,
to watch a red-tail lifting a small rodent away,
to bury our dead ones
in the secret mounds of our hearts.

21

Butterfly

It was better it had worked itself
out this way…unannounced…
rummaging through dusty drawers,
turning over rocks on solitary beaches
for a name that would fit…a sense of waking

to find each thing of this world
had been renewed in your…my image
as we were renewed in each thing's
—what is it—love that begins in an egg
laid in the mud millions of years ago
but this time with care…moves up
to the soul, species through species

…the far fetched bird perched in a live oak
calling out, not of this world yet is
all the same…and how we have melted away
in so many ways and still remain water
floating on water…in

so many places and the same place at
the same time, growing old
—I see you there do you see me?   as though
all this time we'd labored to improvise
the right question to ask   and yet
even this is not it: the whole of it…for

after all
I am only old blood: sinews wishing to extend
groping for light (creature and mineral).
Can you feel what I mean, touch it, taste it:
the passing that goes on even without us,
the spiral staircase
we ride descending, ascending
all at the same time?

I dreamed once the earth was a cocoon
waiting to be cracked open. The colors—greens,
rubies, the yellows, the blues—had come alive
        —organic, sentient—
glowing in a sea of maternal nothingness.
When I woke, direction were countless centers,
each with its own sense of balance and truth
—its need to be: a fine piece of pottery
thrown and fired—red and green—in need
to be touched.

I've touched
the satin tails of sea creatures
many times my size. We were twins.
I have no name for it—layers of nacre,
mother-of-pearl—that soothe the essential wound
where the child of all children cries alone
and there are no clean linens, no substance,
no milk. I dreamed once

that all the roaches and ants of the world
had souls that swarm in seas of being,
and that we are not necessary—beasts among beasts,
granted a mirror to look in upon ourselves,
and nothing more.

I grieved once for a sorrowing mother
—her loss filled me with the sea.

Sentence Fragment: A Sonnet

As on that day you passed by
a small shallow stream and
the great white egret, poised, stock still,

at one edge, to snatch what nutrition
the running water should bring
slowed time

to a single tick of the clock
so that a blank page would open
to your eyes and be written on:

the footsteps of your passage,
perhaps meaningless, except within
the context of that one eternal moment

as on the day
worlds collapse and a new one begins.

Anhinga: Two Continents... Three Worlds

and...is as it was inscribed
in the encoded Knots (Kipu)
the Three Worlds/the three times
(Kimsa Pachakuna)   and

the Kestrel—joy of mountain children—
like a knot securing the weave, sews
the Upper World to This World
—the Hanan Pacha to Kay Pacha—
brings power to their dreams,
which extends into day   as

toads—peeping through cold Spring Nights—
bind their place of birth in the Under World
—Ucu Pacha—also to this place where
their eggs and semen meld
in a frenzy of flesh
and slime

and here/now, this Tupi anhinga
—snake bird—fisher of pools
and deep rivers, master of soaring flight,
balances its precarious chances
on a slim limb of a tree by the shore
of Lake Maggiore, offering
its waterlogged feathers to the sun:

voyager through
these three Sacred Worlds/these three Sacred Times:
Kay kimsa Sumaq Pachakuna,
Kay kimsa Mumaq Pachakuna

Paul Eppling's Armadillos

I

A YouTube video scans over
this confabulation of machine and auto parts
all placed—as you recall the pond…its luxury
of palms, oaks, myrtles, and pines—
in the right place. Chrome bumpers become

the front and hind armored quarters
of what nature evolved from keratin and bone:
the untoward creature that now confronts you
—or you confront—the size of a large Indian
rhinoceros, which brings to mind
                Dürer's 1515 woodcut
                        or
a hornless triceratops, the skeleton of which
stopped you cold in amazement at that first walk
through a natural history museum (how old
were you…ten? Maybe 11?)

as if the mass and weight
of the inorganic had become organic
to mirror on a hyperbolic scale
the course of genes through the chancy furnace
of nature that produced
                a tiny armadillo

…and how the coils of an asphalt heater,
welded to the two plates, morph into
the creature's mid-section: an x-ray
reproduced in metal of the its entrails
…and how more metal—steel—pounded and welded
become its fingers
                        even its nails.

II

But you are here
—this is no video—
on the Wax Myrtle Pond Trail
of the Boyd Hill Nature Preserve
face to face, *not with the video of the creature,*
                    rather its twin, the one that you first
"discovered"(isn't a work of art always "discovered"
each time you *see* it?) which brings you back each time.

Eppling, you learn, made two,
virtually the same in the assemblage of disparate parts
…one for the lower side—this one—
and one for the upper…bookends
so to speak, to frame it all
and the sign warning of the danger of alligators…
wrapping the package up
…you might say.

III

If you stare hard enough,
the hole that represents the eye
might draw you into the hollow of the head
—a chamber of silence, of stillness,
you can imagine, of the inner skull
to reach the opposite side, and out
onto a glimpse of the pond
and the life that continues there,
                    What to make of this?

This presence of forged steel;
a small almost circular pond…
                    A single strand
of spider web, vibrating in the sun
to mark the silk trail a spider has taken
as she floated on a slight breeze
from one branch to another…
                    And then, a dragonfly.

IV

Somehow…in some way, it is inevitable…
you come to consider the history of metal…the fortunes
of iron, its birth in the entrails of a molten planet,
itself being born…the ore, blasted and shoveled
from its core, smelted in furnaces that blackened
the skies of restless cities (Pittsburgh, Cleveland);
pounded into machines and auto parts

and melted and pounded once again:

                                        This statue,

its own fables or myths to tell,
that focuses the commotion of living
that goes on all about it;

makes it all hallowed
…sacred, so to speak.

Potsherds and Gators

(The Indigenous People of Florida: In Memoriam)

…and those precarious lives—played out
drop by drop on hammocks that are no more
anchored above cypress swamps that are no more—

whom the sheen of crossed sales, guns and disease
erased, leaving these scraps of memory:
a path leading nowhere here, a shard there

…as of when the bellowing of bull gators
—in rage—in love—woke them from sleep
to a waking myth…and the gator

was more than flesh and leather, but
a sacred coagulate of water, the shape
of time: energy made flesh.

…and there was more: there were pathways
to the gardens of the sea; the potsherds were vessels.
They cooked. They ate. They loved
and raged. Slept and died

—the humdrum of living made flesh, made bone.
And here on this postage stamp nature reserve
where the highway buzz outweighs the flight of birds,

I write letters in my head of remorse
and regret with no one to send them to
—how do we make sherds and gators holy again?

Acknowledgements

I would like to thank the following people for helping me in the preparation of this chapbook.

The people at Boyd Hill Nature Preserve:

Taylor Graham Thornton, Nature Preserve Director

George L. Heinrich, Heinrich Ecological Service

Ginger Platt, who works at the front desk and answered so many questions I had regarding Boyd Hill.

I would also like to thank the members of my writing group for their help and suggestions as I wrote these poems: Sandra Stollman, Marsha Mathews, Cliff Scharke, and Monika Volkhardt.

I want to thank Shara Bunis for her amazing watercolor on the front cover of this chapbook.

Special thanks to Dale Winslow, my publisher, who made the whole thing possible.

About the Author

Vincent Spina is from Brooklyn, NY and now resides in St Petersburg, FL. He received a Ph.D. from New York University in South American Literature with a specialty in Andean culture. He is the author of El modo épico in José María Arguedas. He has written four books of poetry: *Outer Borough*, *Dialogue*, *The Sumptuous Hills of Gulfport*, and *Sundial*. He has also published in various magazines and some of his poems can be heard on "The Poetry Channel".

www.ingramcontent.com/pod-product-compliance
Lightning Source LLC
Chambersburg PA
CBHW031542040426
42445CB00010B/665